GOD'S FINAL EXAM

HOW TO KNOW IF YOU'RE TRULY SAVED

ARE YOU READY FOR WHAT'S NEXT?

WILLIAM BURK

WESTBOW
PRESS®
A DIVISION OF THOMAS NELSON
& ZONDERVAN

WestBow Press books may be ordered through booksellers or by contacting:

WestBow Press
A Division of Thomas Nelson & Zondervan
1663 Liberty Drive
Bloomington, IN 47403
www.westbowpress.com
844-714-3454

Scripture taken from the King James Version of the Bible.

ISBN: 978-1-6642-3197-9 (sc)
ISBN: 978-1-6642-3196-2 (hc)
ISBN: 978-1-6642-3198-6 (e)

Library of Congress Control Number: 2021908308

Print information available on the last page.

WestBow Press rev. date: 05/20/2021

CONTENTS

INTRODUCTION

This book may be one of the most important and unique books you will ever read. It is important because it sets out to answer the question, "How can I know for sure I am truly saved?" It is unique in the fact that it does not set out to teach you how to become saved; it explains how to know you really are. I believe this information makes this book vitally important.

Now, the above question is sometimes communicated differently, as some may ask, "How can I know for sure I will go to heaven when I die?" or "Will I live with God forever?" or "What will happen to me when I die?" The questions are basically the same; it is the answer to those questions that people are looking for. The issue is how I can know, with certainty, I will be okay. So, I am taking the liberty in assuming the reader has, at a bare minimum, made a profession of faith in Jesus as his or her Savior and Lord and he or she believes their salvation is secure. But is your salvation really secure? The purpose of this book is to help you answer that one important question.

The only way to have peace of mind about the answer to our question is to have a correct knowledge of another book, which is by far the most important and unique book you will ever read. That book is the Bible. Throughout its pages, God is informing the reader of his or her need to find the right answer to their questions. Our search for answers is of extreme importance to God too, and because it is, He has supplied the answers we are looking for. In fact, God has provided us with a comprehensive "final exam" to our knowledge of our true salvation in one of His New Testament books contained in His Word. Since an exam is an educational assessment intended to measure one's knowledge, skill, aptitude, or beliefs, God is once again demonstrating His great concern for us by "testing" all of those characteristics in us, so we may know exactly where we stand with God now and what we may expect when we stand before Him in the future. Therefore, God's final exam is meant to reveal to us where we truly stand with Him. He provides the educational resources to increase our knowledge, skills, aptitudes, and beliefs; He also offers us the final exam to see if we're deficient in any of them.

God's comprehensive final exam is found in the biblical book of 1 John. In the book that you are now reading, I have provided a verse by verse commentary of 1 John to help you fully understand and hopefully pass the exam with a high score that would ultimately glorify Jesus.

Reverend William Burk

BACKGROUND

The "epistle" or "letter" of 1 John has a unique style in that it is actually not in the form or style of a letter at all. It has no salutation at the beginning, nor a greeting at its conclusion. Its style is more of a sermon preached to a group of believers. It has all the marks of a message from a devoted pastor who had a love and concern for his flock. I have written this book for the very same reasons.

The writer of this letter, the apostle John, served as pastor of the church in Ephesus, which was founded by Paul. In order to understand the First Epistle of John we must know something about the city of Ephesus at the beginning of the second century. It was very much like your city or hometown today. There were four important factors at the time which prevailed in Ephesus and throughout the Roman world; these factors are prevalent in our society too.

First, there was an easy familiarity with Christianity. Many of the believers were children and grandchildren of the first Christians. The new and bright sheen of the Christian faith had become tarnished. The newness had worn off. The thrill and glory of the first days had faded. But many years later, when the Lord Jesus sent a letter to the Ephesian believers through John while he was in exile on the Island of Patmos, He said, *"Nevertheless I have somewhat against thee, because thou hast left thy first love"* (Rev. 2:4). It was as Jesus had long before warned, *"... because iniquity shall abound, the love of many shall wax cold"* (Matt. 24:12). The Ephesians' devotion and dedication to Christ was at low ebb, and the primary reason was unrepentant sin.

Second, the Ephesians had become "assembly–line" Christians, programmed by the computer of compromise. They had become plastic Christians. They were cast in a different mold from the disciples to whom Jesus had said, *"If ye were of the world, the world would love his own: but because ye are not of the world, but I have chosen you out of the world, therefore the world hateth you"* (John 15:19). And also in His high priestly prayer to His Father are these words: *"I have given them thy word; and the world hath hated them, because they are not of the world, even as I am not of the world"* (John 17:14). There was a breakdown of the Judeo–Christian ethic and a disregard of biblical standards.

Third, the danger to the Ephesian church was not persecution from the outside but seduction from the inside. The Lord Jesus Himself had warned of this: *"For there shall arise false Christs, and false prophets, and shall shew great signs and wonders; insomuch that, if it were possible, they shall deceive the very elect"* (Matt. 24:24). And the apostle Paul had said to the Ephesian elders: *"For I know this, that after my departing shall grievous wolves enter in among you, not sparing the flock. Also of your own selves shall men arise, speaking perverse things, to draw away disciples after them"* (Acts 20:29–30).

Fourth, Christianity was not in danger of being destroyed; it was in danger of being changed. The attempt was being made to improve it, give it intellectual respectability, and let it speak in the terms of the popular philosophies of the day. The only problem with that was it did not work. It will not work today either.

The real enemy to Christianity then and now is false teaching about Christianity. The main issue John addressed in his letter was the false teaching of "Gnosticism," which was the basic philosophy of the Roman Empire, and I am afraid to say, it is the basic philosophy of the world right now.

Gnosticism, in its simplest form, is the belief that man is basically good. Therefore, given enough training, time, and resources, man can "fix" himself. The same principle is in modern liberalism which maintains that there is a spark of good in everyone and that, given enough "resources" (dollars), each person is to develop that spark of good. The Bible teaches a very different ideology and one which I believe is extremely more accurate.

1 John has been called the "holy of holies" of the New Testament. It takes the child of God across the threshold into the fellowship

of the Father's home. It is the family epistle. Paul's epistles and all the other epistles are church epistles, but this is a family epistle and should be treated that way.

The church is a body of believers in the position where we are blessed "...*with all spiritual blessings in the heavenlies in Christ*" (Eph. 1:3). We are given that position when we believe in the Lord Jesus Christ. Believing in the Lord Jesus brings us into the family of God. In the family, we have a relationship which can be broken but is restored when "we confess our sins." Then *"he is faithful and just to forgive us our sins, and to cleanse us from all unrighteousness"* (1 John 1:9).

1 John is usually the book which I preach from when I begin my ministry in a new church. I am convinced that this epistle is more important for believers in the church than the church epistles. To the reader who believes he or she is going to heaven one day, let me boldly say, it is very important to understand this short book.

THE THREE DELUSIONS

In the opening verses of the book of 1 John, the author confirms his credentials as one whose witness and testimony should be accepted and assimilated. As you read his words, think about how passionate he is with his subject matter. We need to understand why too. Soon the Bible will confront us with three strong delusions that have plagued humankind from its beginning and affect each new generation. These delusions are very important to our understanding of why God writes this letter through the pen of John. We should all pay very close attention.

> *That which was from the beginning, which we have heard, which we have seen with our eyes, which we have looked upon, and our hands have handled, of the Word of life; (For the life was manifested, and we have seen it, and bear witness, and shew unto you that eternal life, which was with the Father, and was manifested unto*

us;) That which we have seen and heard declare we unto you, that ye also may have fellowship with us: and truly our fellowship is with the Father, and with his Son Jesus Christ. And these things write we unto you, that your joy may be full. (1 John 1:1–4)

In these opening verses, the apostle John gets right to the point: God has sent His Son, who has always existed, into the world, and John was a credible eyewitness to what he is about to record. John and many others actually saw Jesus, heard Him teach, and touched Him as He lived and ministered on earth. John is adamant that he is a legitimate spokesperson for Jesus and that his testimony is true. Since John was an eyewitness, I want to know his testimony, and I have no reason to doubt it.

In 1 Corinthians 15:3–8, Paul gives a list of people to whom the risen Jesus appeared. These witnesses to the resurrected Jesus include the apostle Peter, James the brother of Jesus, John, and, most intriguingly, a group of more than five hundred people at the same time. What fair and impartial judge or court would not consider the testimony of over five hundred eyewitnesses as absolutely credible? What person, confronted with the testimony of over five hundred eyewitnesses to an event, would ignore it? I would say no one. Yet millions do regarding the validity of the resurrected Jesus. Do you understand why? Since the message of the gift of Christ is so beautiful, since the facts of His death and resurrection are so incredibly dynamic, and as the blessings offered are so impelling, one wonders how it is that rational people can neglect coming to the Redeemer. How is such foolishness to be explained? Let's consider several possibilities.

First, some are simply unaware that they are lost. The Bible teaches that Christ came to seek and save the lost (Luke 19:10). Unless a person is aware of being lost, he or she will see no need whatsoever for Christ as a Savior. Another great reason to attend a true church where sin is still dealt with biblically in the pulpit.

For many decades society has been told by rationalist philosophers and humanistic psychologists that sin does not exist in reality. It is alleged to be the mere imaginative concoction of insecure, religious fanatics. Humans do not sin, they are just involved in "unacceptable behavior."

Until the message of sin, rebellion, and yes, guilt can be burned into the consciences of spiritually lost people, many will continue to see absolutely no need for what Jesus Christ has to offer.

Second, some will not come to Christ because they are not convinced of His uniqueness. There was a time when most of our neighbors revered the name of Jesus. But that day is rapidly vanishing. We are living in an increasingly unbelieving world. Many Americans no longer even believe in the existence of God. They have been taught from elementary school onward, and via the modern media outlets, that the universe is eternal and self-sustaining. Again, we are taught that humans evolved from an animal ancestry. They say the Bible is not the Word of God, but that it is merely a collection of ancient fables. And Jesus Christ, though He may have been a remarkable teacher and a benevolent influence of antiquity, nonetheless, is not the unique Son of God and the Savior of the world. My friend, without an accurate knowledge of who Christ is, no one will ever be drawn to Him.

Third, some do not come to the Lord because, due to false teaching, they have concluded that they are already associated with Him. In Acts 19, one can read of certain "strolling Jews" who pretended to have the ability to cast out evil spirits. Part of their exorcism routine was to invoke the name of Christ. But they were dramatically exposed as fakes. There is something we can learn from this case: not everyone who claims connection with Jesus Christ actually enjoys such a union. I think this is a biblical truth that some of us need to be reminded of. Correct teaching and an accurate understanding of the message must precede obedience to the gospel.

Fourth, some will not come to Jesus because they are unwilling to pay the price He requires. If one would follow Christ, one must be willing to forsake all that is in conflict with heaven's requirements. A person must be willing to deny himself or herself, take up the cross daily, and follow the Lord (Luke 9:23). The Savior urged men and women to count the cost before assuming the role of discipleship, and he or she who is not willing to renounce any obstacle to the faith cannot be a follower of Christ (Luke 14:25–35).

For some, forsaking worldliness is too great of a demand for discipleship (2 Tim. 4:10). Others cannot afford the time, so they trade the few moments of time for eternity. The excuses are many; the result is the same. Other priorities crowd out our true relationship with Christ.

Fifth, some will not come to the Lord because they fear failure. I have heard the excuse many times: "I would become a Christian. But I know I just couldn't hold out." Do you not realize that when you turn to Christ you are but a babe in the faith? Don't we understand that heaven is sympathetic to human frailty? Hasn't Jesus promised to be with us "all the days" (Matt. 28:20)?

Yes, we will make mistakes—and frequently. But we will repent of those things and learn to grow in spite of our blunders. What if one reasoned: "I will not marry because so many marriages end in divorce"? Surely that would be unsound thinking. What if the farmer argued: "I will not plant, for there was a crop failure last year"? He (and others) would go hungry!

Don't fear failure. Do your best to serve your God. And promise yourself to be progressively learning and responding to the truth.

Sixth, and perhaps saddest of all, some do not come to Christ because of what they see in professed Christians. Look, no one will be excused for his or her own disobedience on the Day of Judgment because he or she was influenced by someone else's bad example. Each person is responsible for their own activity (2 Cor. 5:10). Be that as it may, it is a fact that cannot be denied: some of the Lord's own people are His worst enemies. By their coarse and wretched lives, they drive away many from the truth even before they have opportunity to know the gospel.

Yes, there are many excuses why people reject Christ, but there are no legitimate reasons!

Returning to our study, John presents us with absolute facts about Jesus. These facts are important because John also gives us great hope in knowing we, too, may have fellowship with Jesus and God through the same relationship John had. The opportunity to see, hear, and touch Jesus physically is no longer available, but one can certainly do these things spiritually now, and that's exactly what John is describing here. Fellowship with the Son and the Father is possible, but it must be a biblical fellowship—meaning we must come to both in the manner they have prescribed. There is no other way. Once this requirement has been met, our true joy may be full. This joy is a spiritual and eternal joy; the only real, lasting joy there is.

This then is the message which we have heard of him, and declare unto you, that God is light, and in him is no darkness at all. If we say that we have fellowship with him, and walk in darkness, we lie, and do not the truth: But if we walk in the light, as he is in the light, we have fellowship one with another, and the blood of Jesus Christ his Son cleanseth us from all sin. If we say that we have no sin, we deceive ourselves, and the truth is not in us. If we confess our sins, he is faithful and just to forgive us our sins, and to cleanse us from all unrighteousness. If we say that we have not sinned, we make him a liar, and his word is not in us. (1 John 1:5–10)

Here is the message John is providing in this first chapter: God is holy! John has seen it, he has witnessed it, he has learned it, and he has shared it, and this revelation has changed his life. Jesus is holy and in Him there is nothing unholy. This incredible fact of holiness is vitally important. It is the basis on which God tests a person—that is, the person's own holiness. So we need to study this deeper to prepare for the upcoming tests.

The word "darkness" in the Bible describes both the state and works of a person. It symbolizes evil and sin, everything that life should not be, and everything that a person should not do. Darkness is ignorance of God and His teachings. Darkness is the influence of a fallen world and Satan. Darkness is evil behavior

WILLIAM BURK

and deeds. Darkness is our spiritual condition for all eternity unless light replaces it. Our own spiritual darkness is primarily why we struggle with Jesus in the first place.

The thing about darkness is, it should scare us. From the time we are young children, darkness is a frightening concept. For many of us, the fear of darkness never departs. But while the Bible speaks of darkness hundreds of times, it is never glorified or celebrated. The Bible regards darkness as something we should all avoid at all costs and, from the earliest of passages, gives us indications that darkness is a scary thing. For example, in Genesis 15:12, the Bible records: *"And when the sun was going down, a deep sleep fell upon Abram; and, lo, a horror of great darkness fell upon him."* Here, as in many other verses in the Bible, darkness is described as a horror. Do you better understand the significance of the word "darkness" now?

This is why in John 8:12, Jesus said, *"I am the light of the world: he that followeth me shall not walk in darkness, but shall have the light of life."* You see, darkness is used mostly to describe the idea of separation with God; for if one is walking in darkness, one is walking separated from God. If that's not remedied, then the next level of biblical darkness described in the Bible refers to the unrepentant being cast out into outer darkness, or Hell. I do not want anyone to go there; I trust you do not either.

8

So what John learned in Jesus' graduate theology class, he now declares: God is holy and the very opposite of unholiness is darkness. God's holiness outshines the darkness of man's soul. God's holiness outperforms the enemy's best efforts. God's holiness illuminates the darkness of a fallen world. Jesus is light and has no darkness (sin) in Him at all. He is the one who is the ultimate in trustworthiness. His testimony is the truest of all. His way is the truth; His life is the truth; His message is the truth. This is what John is describing here. But John now transitions to verse 6 and immediately challenges the reader as he confronts three common delusions many people have, mostly because they walk in darkness. The rest of chapter one will be used to counterpoint these delusions.

"If we say that we have fellowship with him, and walk in darkness, we lie, and do not the truth" (1 John 1:6). The first delusion is found here in verse 6. Many people truly believe they can walk in sin and still have fellowship with God. In fact, this attitude is so prevalent in western Christianity now that it may never be eliminated before the return of Jesus. Look, Jesus came to provide a way for humankind to have a *true* relationship with God again, not a blank check to sin. I don't see how this could be any plainer or more encouraging to those walking in darkness. God is telling every person who claims to be saved that if he or she says they are saved but still live in sin, then they are lying to themselves, and ultimately trying to lie to God. But

of course God knows better and refuses to be fooled. What's our hope? Let's look at verse 7.

"But if we walk in the light, as he is in the light, we have fellowship one with another, and the blood of Jesus Christ his Son cleanseth us from all sin" (1 John 1:7). Here is a contractual if/then statement from God. *If* we walk as Jesus walked, *then* we have fellowship. If we don't, we won't. It is honestly just that simple. A person cannot have fellowship with God and be content to walk in sin. A person can think they can; they can wish they can; they can even ignore His Word and do their own thing, but God's Word says they cannot walk in sin and have fellowship with Him.

However, if we turn from darkness and walk in the light of Jesus' freedom, example, and teachings, we may rest assured we are in fellowship with God and all others who are doing the same. But going deeper, God tells us an amazing and frightening truth: we must live our lives holy unto the Lord if we expect the blood of Jesus to cleanse us. This is a critical point to note. When we walk in the light of Christ, God sees our sins covered by His blood. He accepts us as being in Christ, and our sins are forgiven. Therefore, the believer is to walk in fellowship with Jesus all day, every day. This willingness is a total game changer. The next three verses are game changers too, and they point out the second delusion.

"If we say that we have no sin, we deceive ourselves, and the truth is not in us. If we confess our sins, he is faithful and just to forgive us our sins, and to cleanse us from all unrighteousness. If we say that we have not sinned, we make him a liar, and his word is not in us" (1 John 1: 8–10). The second delusion many people suffer from is the false idea he or she is not totally sinful and depraved. The world's attempt to brush this off and the human thought process that a person is not totally depraved and sinful, is a great misconception. Read what John also wrote in the Gospel of John:

> *And this is the condemnation, that the light has come into the world, and men loved darkness rather than light, because their deeds were evil. For everyone practicing evil hates the light and does not come to the light, lest his deeds should be exposed. But he who does the truth comes to the light, that his deeds may be clearly seen, that they have been done in God.* (John 3:19–21)

The idea that we are all okay and that somehow it will all work out is a work of darkness. Furthermore, notice the word "sin" is singular and not plural. It speaks to the root of what humankind really is. These verses prove the point. For a person to say he or she has no sin is deceived according to the Word of God. Every person ever born has a sinful nature. For a person to deny that is quite the height of hypocrisy. The Bible teaches if we think that way, we are allowing darkness to overcome our thinking. It goes further by saying the truth is not in us.

On the surface, this may not seem like that big of a deal. But if Jesus is the truth, and because of deception the truth is not in us, we're in trouble (John 14:6). The key to overcoming the darkness is found in our confessions of who we really are and of what we are really guilty. If we confess our sins, Jesus is faithful to forgive and cleanse us from our sins. So true confession must be connected to truly living in the light. Confession, or the acknowledgement of sin to God, is extremely important and infinitely valuable. But, we must not stop there, for it is also the acknowledgment of our sins to another person whom we have wronged (James 5:16). Both are necessary for forgiveness and cleansing. Confessing to only one party is guaranteeing a maximum score of only fifty percent on this test. That is a failing grade no matter what school one is in.

Verse 10 goes even further with this concept and addresses the third common delusion: *"If we say that we have not sinned, we make him a liar, and his word is not in us."* Many people wrongly believe they can become righteous and sinless on their own. If they love better than everyone else, or if they work at the church, or if they don't do what everyone is doing, they will be in good standing with God. If this is true, the death of Jesus was unwarranted. God pulls no punches here and informs us if a person says they have not sinned (or not sinned much), we are calling Him a liar. Why? Because He has written all have sinned and are in darkness (Romans 3:23). Calling God a liar puts a person in a very precarious situation. I am sure I don't have to provide any further comment on it. When a person sins, there is a prescribed methodology to get back right with God. I would say failing at this would be totally unnecessary and unacceptable. But flagrant and habitual sin is the darkest form of darkness and often leads a person to being unrepentant, unconfessional, and uncaring (Matthew 24:12), and that, in my opinion, is what is very common in our lives today.

The simple truth is we must be repentant and confessional continuously. A person is deceived if he or she denies that he or she is a sinner and has sinned. But Jesus came to *forgive our sins*, meaning God has forgiven us of the guilt we bear, if we repent and confess, so we can now stand before Him. Jesus also came to *cleanse us from all unrighteousness* meaning God has decontaminated us from ourselves when we are repentant and confessional. How do we know this for sure? God has proclaimed it in His Word. He is faithful and righteous. But, one must follow the prescribed methodology. Our non-biblical ideas, practices, traditions, and habits are not going to pass the tests.

We are about to begin the testing God has for us in the next chapters. The purpose for these following tests is to show us any weaknesses in our knowledge of biblical principles and application of God's Word. There are no tests like these tests in comparison, nor in importance, to the true believer. In fact, the tests will uncover whether or not a person is a true believer! I would imagine there is nothing more important to know. Let us begin.

TEST 1 - DO I REALLY KNOW GOD?

Many people are curious to know if they really know God, and here God gives them a way to know for sure. One of the most common realities in the so-called believer's life is saying they know God, but the way they live their lives speaks differently. To make it more personal, do you really know God, or just know facts about God? Do you really know what His Word says and live it, or do you know what makes you feel good and fake it? Do you get your theology from the shallow ponds of misinformation or from the depths of God's well? Well, let's see what the test proves.

Chapter 2 of 1 John is very thorough, dealing with the terribleness of sin and the effect it has on the world. Unfortunately, many people say they have not sinned. Some even believe they can become righteous on their own; they do not need Jesus' help.

They object to the idea the Son of God had to die for their sins. They object to the preaching of sin, that they are sinners, and that God has issues with all of it. They are fooled. I encourage you to not be fooled too.

This chapter contains the first of the four "tests" in God's final exam concerning true knowledge of Him. As we study these verses, we should honestly evaluate ourselves to help determine where we really are in our walk with Jesus. If the grade is low, count that as a blessing that now the truth is known, and perhaps there is a need for some remedial training in order to do better. But remember this: God does not grade on a curve, but He will grade on a Cross. One can't take advantage of His grace in doing this. That is foolishness and more darkness. God has made provisions for us if we will respond to Him biblically.

"My little children, these things write I unto you, that ye sin not. And if any man sin, we have an advocate with the Father, Jesus Christ the righteous:" (1 John 2:1). Verse 1 informs us that God is speaking to those who say they are truly saved. John addresses the reader as *"my little children"* and refers to the people who were very dear to him and certainly professing faith in Jesus. Obviously, they were talking the talk but not walking the walk, or there would be no need for the letter. The first verse also simply states the very obvious: while believers are sinful, they should not sin (*that ye sin not*). So God writes *these things* of what he has previously

written in this letter to exhort them in the areas where they needed strength.

John is not teaching perfection here; he's teaching obedience. No one will ever be perfect, and certainly John knows this. God is using John to write His message of spiritual obedience because that is where the power in the fellowship with God resides. If God's grace is the oil that lubricates the machinery, our obedience is that which allows the machinery to work.

"And he is the propitiation for our sins: and not for ours only, but also for the sins of the whole world" (1 John 2:2). For the true believer who is walking with Jesus daily (walking in the Light), there is the advocacy of the forgiving attribute of Christ. The Bible states it is available to the whole world, yet it still must be claimed individually in the manner in which God states it to be claimed. We must remember: we must not take God's grace for granted. We cannot expect forgiveness for sins if we blatantly sin because of God's grace. I addressed that fallacy in my first book, *Conforming to His Image.*

"And hereby we do know that we know him, if we keep his commandments" (1 John 2:3) Our first test helps us to record our level of knowledge of God and our performance with that knowledge. Unfortunately, we live in a day when many people are not interested in knowing God. There is spiritual apathy and complacency in Christian circles too which would lead one

to believe God is not the most important thing in their lives. God knew this would be the case, so He is offering us this test to help us see if we are failing.

How do I know I truly know God? God goes straight to the point here. He clearly says that one of the first proofs that a person truly knows Him is the person will keep His Word. All of it. Not just the popular part of a particular time period in our history, but all of it. This is extremely challenging and personal. This must mean that a person must know His Word well enough to be able to follow it. With this in mind, I think it best that we challenge ourselves personally now.

Let's start off by asking if you truly know His Word well enough to keep it. If you do not, do you know others who do and follow their lead? Verse 3 could not be any plainer. *Do you live a God pleasing, biblical life?* Daily? It's a yes or no answer.

Are there spiritual dead areas in your life? Are you content to be apathetic, and do you think that's okay with God? Do you make excuses for your low performance? Have you settled for mediocrity in your spiritual walk? Are you following what the world says is okay, even though it is in direct opposition to what God says is okay? Are you convinced God is just going to let you slide?

Let's go deeper. Galatians 3:3 states, *"Are ye so foolish? having begun in the Spirit, are ye now made perfect by the flesh?"* To restate this in today's vernacular, I would put it this way: *"Have you gone completely crazy? If obeying the world never led you to Christ, do you think trying to obey the world now will make you a better Christian?"* This is why obeying God's commands is so important. Doing so makes one a better Christian. Being a better Christian makes testing on being a better Christian much easier. Do you see this?

We could possibly get around verse 3 if we had the nerve to do so. But then there's verse 4 staring us right in the face: *"He that saith, I know him, and keepeth not his commandments, is a liar, and the truth is not in him."* This one is going to hurt. If a person says he or she is saved, but doesn't live biblically, daily demonstrating he or she is saved, the Bible is calling them a liar. I'm not; the Bible is. If a person claims to be born-again, yet there's no proof of a conversion by a changed life, God calls this person a liar. If a person claims to be a child of the light, yet is content to live in darkness, the Bible calls him or her a liar. Furthermore, the Bible says there may be a deeper, more detrimental issue present – *the truth is not in them*. Remember, Jesus stated He is the truth. Hard medicine for sure.

What is meant by keeping His commandments? It's knowing what the Bible says and living it out in personal worship to Jesus. All of it. The beginning point is found in Jesus' teaching in Mark chapter 12:30-31:

Jesus answered him, 'And you shall love the Lord your God with all your heart, with all your soul, with all your mind, and with all your strength.' This is the first commandment. And the second, like it, is this: 'You shall love your neighbor as yourself.' There is no other commandment greater than these.

There is much more to God's Word than just this, but if we could be obedient to this, we would be doing quite well at test time.

Is God really that serious? What do you think? Do you love Jesus more than anything else? Is He the most important entity in your life? Is His Word the most important book in your life? Let's take a quick look to see how serious we really are. The true follower of Christ is commanded to attend corporate worship services (Heb 10:25). He or she is commanded to forgive (Col. 3:13). He or she is commanded to evangelize (Mt. 28:19-20). He or she is commanded to give (Mt. 6:2). He or she is commanded to love (John 13:34-35). He or she is commanded to speak truth (Eph. 4:25). And the list goes on and on. So, the test is: Do I attend services? Do I forgive? Do I evangelize? Do I give? Do I love? Do I speak the truth? As imperfect as I may be, am I obedient to God's guidance regarding these and other issues as contained in His Word? Or am I good at making excuses? Excuses will never excuse failing the test.

"But whoso keepeth his word, in him verily is the love of God perfected: hereby know we that we are in him. He that saith he abideth in him ought himself also so to walk, even as he walked" (1 John 2:5–6). The next part of the test is found in these verses. Read what it says. We once again are reminded that we know the love of God is perfected by the one who keeps His Word. Verse 6 records the call for obedience. If a person says they are saved, the least they can do is to walk in the light as Jesus did. In fact, the Holy Spirit will insist on this! Again, if a person is going to talk about it, they should at least walk it. The truly obedient Christian, the one who will do well on God's final exam, is the one who purposely and obediently walks in the manner prescribed by God daily. This lifestyle attitude will continue until He calls the person home. No excuses, just execution. A truly born-again person will at some point become a biblically-responsible person. If not, there is a good chance they were really never born-again in the first place.

"Brethren, I write no new commandment unto you, but an old commandment which ye had from the beginning. The old commandment is the word which ye have heard from the beginning" (1 John 2:7). Our third test question under the heading of knowing God is now presented to us. John starts out by explaining to the reader that the curriculum has never changed. God is saying this has been the expectation since the beginning. What is this expectation? The expectation is that the true believer will love their fellow humans.

"Again, a new commandment I write unto you, which thing is true in him and in you: because the darkness is past, and the true light now shineth" (1 John 2:8). If a person is truly saved, darkness and dark living will be a thing of the past at some point. There should be a new light shining in a person's life. If it is not there, there is something fundamentally wrong. God brings the message into clarity by challenging the believer to examine his or her love for other believers. To live in a condition of hatred or dislike of another Kingdom resident is a dead giveaway the person is still walking blindly in the dark.

"He that saith he is in the light, and hateth his brother, is in darkness even until now" (1 John 2:9). The word "hateth" as used here means to "detest someone to the point of persecution." It points out that when we are mean-spirited to another believer, we are walking in darkness. Have you ever been mean or hateful to another believer? Have you never confessed and repented to God *and* the other person? No? You are failing the test. And knowing that now and still refusing to do it will cause problems you really do not want.

"He that loveth his brother abideth in the light, and there is none occasion of stumbling in him" (1 John 2:10). Here, the Bible describes one who is passing the test because of their obedience to God's commandments. The person who abides in Christ will have a new found love for other believers. Because of this biblical love, a person now has no need to stumble. He or she has no

reason to be tripped up in his or her walk of faith. Loving our "brother" is passing this part of the test as this demonstrates a heart to draw closer to, and mature in, Jesus.

"But he that hateth his brother is in darkness, and walketh in darkness, and knoweth not whither he goeth, because that darkness hath blinded his eyes" (1 John 2:11). In great contrast, the Bible records that the person who is failing this part of the test is totally lost in the darkness of this world. Several things are mentioned in this verse. First, the person walks in darkness or lives a life of sin. Because of this, he or she has no real direction in life. This person will be concerned with getting all he or she can from the world and its inhabitants. They are driven more by pleasure, comforts, and possessions. Therefore, not loving others is of no consequence to them. The root cause of this condition is spiritual blindness.

"I write unto you, little children, because your sins are forgiven you for his name's sake. I write unto you, fathers, because ye have known him that is from the beginning. I write unto you, young men, because ye have overcome the wicked one. I write unto you, little children, because ye have known the Father" (1 John 2:12–13). Here is something interesting. John writes to three groups of people here: *Little children, fathers, and young men.* But notice the verb tense change. In the earlier verses, John wrote, "*I have written,*" and here he writes, "*I am writing*". The writings point quite strongly to John identifying and writing to the various stages of the spiritual

growth of people in the church. John is simply driving home a very important biblical fact: true believers, no matter what stage of spiritual growth they may be in, must always grow even more in Christ. When you read the two sets of verses side-by-side, you will see exactly what John is doing.

So here begins the third question as it relates to our knowing God test: are you growing spiritually? Is growing and maturing spiritually important to you? Has Jesus grown and matured you since you made a profession of faith? If you really know Jesus, then you will have grown in that knowledge by the very act of being discipled and mature. Have you?

The point is very simple. If we are honest and truthful with ourselves, we will understand that if we truly know Jesus, we will constantly grow in our knowledge of Him. Have you not grown? Are you content with just getting out of hell some day in the future? Are you easily fooled by the world's theology that stands opposed to His theology? Do you not know the difference? Well, then you are failing this part of the test.

"I have written unto you, fathers, because ye have known him that is from the beginning. I have written unto you, young men, because ye are strong, and the word of God abideth in you, and ye have overcome the wicked one" (1 John 2:14). This verse continues with the third test question on the "Do I Really Know God" section of the exam, which is "Is growing in God's Word important to me?"

Is being more Christ-like a goal for my life? Is stepping out of spiritual childish things something I want to continuously do?

So, God classifies the stages of spiritual growth. It would be okay to fail a graduate exam if one was of kindergarten age. In fact, no one would expect anything less. It would also be okay if, spiritually speaking, one was the spiritual equivalent of a high-school student struggling with passing said exam. But if a person has been around long enough to develop spiritual maturity yet fails at the exam, something is inherently wrong.

Spiritual "*little children*" know enough to know their sins are forgiven through Jesus. But what is necessary for all little children is to grow up. An infant in diapers and carrying a bottle is generally considered to be cute and perfectly normal. An adult in diapers and carrying a bottle is a totally different concept. But this is exactly what happens to so many spiritual infants. They never mature in their knowledge of and walk with the Lord. They are content to remain in spiritual diapers, drinking milk and not maturing and putting on the righteous robes of Jesus (Rev. 19:7-8) and eating the meat of the Word (1 Cor. 3:1-3). They know their sins are forgiven, and they also know that is all that matters to them. They are totally missing out on the abundance of Christ now.

John informs us we overcome all darkness by being spiritually strong and knowing and following all of God's Word. Spiritual immaturity can never accomplish this. It is no different than a kindergartener trying to succeed in graduate school. The chances for failure at that point are quite impressive and evident.

"Love not the world, neither the things that are in the world. If any man love the world, the love of the Father is not in him" (1 John 2:15). These verses are the fourth part of the "Do I Really Know God" exam. The Bible is declaring that if a person loves the world or the things of the world more than they love God, then God is not in him or her. This is shocking! God has just told the reader if anything comes before Him, He's not there.

So, do we love the world? If we do, according to the Bible, we do not truly know God. No matter what a person may think or feel, no matter what the guru on television says, no matter what well-meaning friends tell us, we do not truly know God if the world is more important to us. And if we don't know Him, how will we ever make it to heaven?

Let us reason this out. Can we not appreciate and enjoy God's creation? Can we not appreciate the beauty and splendor of our world? Can we not admire God's handiwork? Of course we can, and we should. But we must not fall into the trap of loving the possessions of the world more than we love God. The true believer, the one who can pass the final exam with flying colors, understands that this world is darkness. It is corruptible and passing away (Mt. 24:35). It will eventually be destroyed (2

Peter 3:10). We should desire a heavenward relationship with God far more than earthward experience in this world. Our eyes and minds should be on Jesus.

"For all that is in the world, the lust of the flesh, and the lust of the eyes, and the pride of life, is not of the Father, but is of the world" (1 John 2:16). Interestingly, these three temptations are exactly the same three temptations the devil tempted Adam and Eve with in the Old Testament and Jesus with in the New Testament. One should not be surprised then if the enemy tempts us with the exact same tactics. The Bible clearly teaches when we fall for these three temptations, we are failing the test. Adam and Eve failed it, too, but Jesus did not. Our example is Jesus. He defeated the tactics by truly knowing what God said. Adam and Eve misquoted God. Is there any importance to the contrast? Yes, because within these two sentences are found the examples of failure and passing with flying colors. Do you see it?

Why does God want you to know His Word? Because the enemy will try to use it to tempt you. Temptation almost always begins by distorting authority. This was the approach Satan used when he came to Eve in the garden and with Jesus in the wilderness. Since the Bible is God's authoritative Word, the enemy distorts it in his efforts to use it against us.

"And the world passeth away, and the lust thereof: but he that doeth the will of God abideth forever" (1 John 2:17). The true believer,

in order to pass this part of the test, must not be so enamored with the world's (enemy's) temptations that he or she becomes desensitized to God's commands and expectations. The mature believer should not be enticed to go into unnecessary debt. He or she should not be covetous for things. He or she should not be so earthly minded they are no heavenly good. Why? Because the earth is only temporary. We are too. But doing Kingdom-centered work will last forever. Studying, preparing, and living for eternity is what God expects from His truly born-again people. Disobedience will always fail; obedience will carry us through to graduating at the head of our class.

"Little children, it is the last time: and as ye have heard that antichrist shall come, even now are there many antichrists; whereby we know that it is the last time" (1 John 2:18). Here is the fifth test in this chapter. Do we know enough of God's truths to stay away from false teachings about God's truths? Are we solid in our theology? Are we easily swayed by the opinions of humankind? Are we easy prey to the "isms" of this world? Here is an immutable truth: anything that is against Jesus is against Him or anti-Christ. Anything that is against God, His Word, His true church, is anti-Christ. Any person who falls for any of the teaching that goes against Scripture is anti-Christ. If that's you or someone you know, you or they have just failed this part of the test.

Now, John is still being tender by calling his readers *"little children."* But God again does not want them to stay that way.

He warns us that if we really know Him, we should be able to spot an imposter a mile away, and false teachers are everywhere.

"They went out from us, but they were not of us; for if they had been of us, they would no doubt have continued with us: but they went out, that they might be made manifest that they were not all of us" (1 John 2:19). Here is a shocking statement of the origins of many false teachers: they come from within the *church*. They were within the church, but they were not true believers. They professed Christ, got baptized, joined the church, and became teachers and even ministers; however, they were not true believers. Sadly, this condition is still present in today's church. No matter the good work they may proclaim to do, they failed the test. In essence, they were posers.

When people leave the church because they're angry at the church or its leadership, they are acting improperly. When a person leaves for any reason other than providentially being led to serve elsewhere, there will not be a smooth transition. Unfortunately, it's usually because the person has been hurt emotionally or has been challenged ideologically, and instead of growing through the experience, they run from it.

"But ye have an unction from the Holy One, and ye know all things" (1 John 2:20). True followers have an anointing from the Holy Spirit for true service; one which always glorifies Jesus. False teachers almost always are motivated to serve for their own

ill-gotten gains. Often, we think of actual teachers within the church as the guilty party. But let's get personal again. Have you ever left the church because you didn't agree with something, even though it was biblical? Or maybe it was just a misunderstanding, but you wouldn't reconcile? Have you spread negative gossip about the experience? Have you ever knowingly or unknowingly influenced others to not attend church or stray from God due to your influence on them? Well, if you have, you have failed this part of the test. Why? Because it's not just what we teach from a curriculum or an ideology that counts. It is what we do or don't do, too. How we live in front of others often has more of a lasting impression on the mind-set of other people than what we say. Those people with an "unction" or an anointing of the Holy Spirit will know better.

"I have not written unto you because ye know not the truth, but because ye know it, and that no lie is of the truth" (1 John 2:21). John proclaims that his readers had known the truth, or at least were exposed to it at some point. How does God give a believer real truth? He gives us real truth through the Living Jesus, who is the Living Truth. He also gives us His written Word, the Bible, which is truth too.

This lays a tremendous responsibility on all true followers. We must not just make a profession that we know Jesus; we must also study and search His Word to be taught deeper and important additional truth. We must therefore be studious and diligent in learning and mastering our subject matter, as all good students must do. Paying our fees and taking our "C's" may suffice in Calculus class, but eternal things are eternally more important, and Jesus deserves academic scholars who can pass His tests.

"Who is a liar but he that denieth that Jesus is the Christ? He is antichrist, that denieth the Father and the Son" (1 John 2:22). Two terrible things are said about the person who has an "anti-Christ" spirit. First, they are liars. Second, they are deniers. Lies and denial are two of the main characteristics of people who failed the test.

"Whosoever denieth the Son, the same hath not the Father: (but) he that acknowledgeth the Son hath the Father also" (1 John 2:23). God's Word proclaims that anyone who denies His Word is a liar. Anyone who denies the written Word (the Bible) or the living Word (Jesus) are liars and have the spirit of "antichrist" in them. This is very bold teaching and probably offended many people at the time. It still offends many people even today. But honestly, they also had no excuses then; we have no excuses today either.

God now proceeds to the sixth question of this exam.

"Let that therefore abide in you, which ye have heard from the beginning. If that which ye have heard from the beginning shall remain in you, ye

also shall continue in the Son, and in the Father" (1 John 2:24). How do I know I really know God? Here is the sixth question for this test. Does truth really abide in you? How we live demonstrates if we know Him better than anything else we can do. God's Word will be publically lived out by the true believer because the true believer will always have the Word of God in his or her heart.

John writes to his audience to inform them that they know the truth, or at least they have been exposed to it, and they should always allow it to abide in them. In doing so, they are providing evidence that they are true believers and they truly know God. This truth has also withstood the test of time from the beginning. The Gospel of Jesus Christ will always be the same; it will never change. Is the Gospel of Jesus continuously lived out in your life? Are you carried away with the world's teaching on spirituality? Are we infatuated with worldly pleasures and possessions? Are we lured into the enemy's trap of complacent Christianity? If so, we're failing the test.

"And this is the promise that he hath promised us, even eternal life" (1 John 2:25). In spite of this, verse 25 is an incredibly uplifting verse. God reminds us of the promise of eternal life. But it is not something a person can take for granted or assume it is theirs just because they were baptized years ago. This promise supersedes all other promises, but one must be in this promise

according to biblical directions. Anything short of that is from the spirit of "antichrist" as verse 26 indicates.

"These things have I written unto you concerning them that seduce you" (1 John 2:26). The word "seduce" means "to deceive or lead astray," and this is another characteristic of a false teacher. I know of many people who were very destructive in their departure from church, and they wanted to take as many people with them as possible out of hatred and spite. They got mad at something someone said or something the pastor didn't do, and they caused a mass exodus out of the church. Have you ever done this? Has this ever been done to you?

"But the anointing which ye have received of him abideth in you, and ye need not that any man teach you: but as the same anointing teacheth you of all things, and is truth, and is no lie, and even as it hath taught you, ye shall abide in him" (1 John 2:27). God has protected us by His Spirit who lives in us, as demonstrated here. What is the issue in this verse? A truly born-again believer will have the Holy Spirit to teach and guide them in the study of His Word. A mature believer should be able to spot a false teacher a mile away. I know I sure can. Can you?

"And now, little children, abide in him; that, when he shall appear, we may have confidence, and not be ashamed before him at his coming. If ye know that he is righteous, ye know that every one that doeth righteousness is born of him" (1 John 2:28–29). 1 John chapter

2 ends with our seventh question on our first test, and that is, do I truly abide in Christ? So far, we have been asked to answer six separate questions on this test. First, do I keep all of God's commandments? Second, do I really love my fellow man? Third, am I truly growing spiritually? Fourth, do I love God more than this world? Fifth, do I guard myself from all the false teaching in this world? Sixth, does God's Word truly live in me? Now, does Jesus truly live in me?

For a person to truly abide in Christ, he or she must abide in the very nature of God. He or she lives like God lives and lives life like life should be lived. They live righteously and holy. The word "abide" means to "dwell or stay," and it refers to the believer as being settled on dwelling with Jesus daily. It means the true believer will experience the indwelling presence of God's Holy Spirit. He or she will bear fruit for Jesus. He or she will do the will of God and never settle for anything less. So we are taught we know that we know God by the daily presence of God in our lives and our daily desire to live for Him. Does that describe you? If not, why not?

We are also reminded in these verses that if we are truly abiding in Him, we will not be living in shame, even at His second coming. This can't be true, you say? Everyone will shrink back from Christ because of our sins? Have you not read these verses? Let us get our theology from God's Book and not our fallen hearts. The Bible is clear that some will be joyful at His return because they passed the tests given them, all to the praise of Jesus.

How are you doing so far? Well, I've gotten four of the seven right, so I'm doing okay. Unfortunately, four out of seven is only fifty-seven percent: a failing grade. I have accomplished five of the seven. Well, five divided by seven is only seventy-one percent: barely a passing grade. Six out of seven is only a mid-B. Do we think Jesus is going to be impressed with our lack-luster performance? Would you be?

Those true followers of Jesus, who stopped making excuses and started living righteously, know it is not only possible to do so, they know they live this way because He is righteous. If He lives in them and they abide in Him, and He is righteous, how could they possibly live any other way?

1 John chapter 2 should be a wakeup call for all of us who are either undecided about Jesus or who are living in sin and yet claim to know Him. We can't honestly say we know Him and not obey Him. Whoever knows Him will strive to obey Him; no, not perfectly, but they will be living, reading, and obeying His Word. If not, they will have no confidence on the day of His appearing and it will *become plain that they all are not of us* (1 John 2:19). Make your election and calling sure (2 Pet 1:10), and do this before it is too late (Rev 20:12-15).

How Can I Really Know I Really Know God?

Test One Of God's Final Exam
1 John 2:3-29

Be very honest with your answers. A help would be to answer them the way you think Jesus would answer them about you!

YES NO

1. Do I accurately know God's Word, and do I strive to keep all of it?

2. Do I have a tenderness for the well-being of all people?

3. Am I growing and maturing spiritually?

4. Do I love God more than this world?

5. Do I guard myself from all the false teaching in this world?

6. Is there true evidence that God's written Word truly lives in me?

7. Is there real evidence that Jesus truly lives in me?

Divide your yes responses by 7. This will give you your numeric grade for this test.

91-100% = A Great Job!

81-90% = B Not Bad!

71-80% = C Needs Improvement

61-70% = D Remedial Classes

0-60% = F Not good at all

3

TEST 2 - DO I REALLY LOVE GOD?

We begin a new chapter in our study to do well on God's final exam. In this chapter, we are given an additional six tests to help us determine if we truly love God. The previous chapter helped us with the concept of truly knowing God; now we see if that knowledge has brought us to loving Him.

Is this really important? It certainly is to God. The love of God must be lit and fanned by the knowledge of God, for to know Him is to love Him. The greater our true knowledge of God's love, the more we will adore Him for who He is and want to serve Him. When knowledge of God fuels love to God, we serve and honor Him. In fact, the entire Christian life flows from the knowledge and love of God: *"Grace and peace be multiplied to you in the knowledge of God and of Jesus our Lord; seeing that His divine power has granted to us everything pertaining to life and godliness, through the true knowledge of Him who called us by His own glory and excellence"* (2 Pet. 1:2-3). It truly is important, so let's take our tests.

"Behold, what manner of love the Father hath bestowed upon us, that we should be called the sons of God: therefore the world knoweth us not, because it knew him not" (1 John 3:1). Behold the manner of love God has for His truly saved people. This is quite incredible. If God truly loves us this much, it means He is not far off from us or indifferent to our plight. No, God loves us with an indescribable love; a love so dynamic and strong He is willing to adopt the believer into His own family. The true believer is now a son or a daughter of the Great King. How phenomenal is that? But the issue here is not the reality of God's love for His children. The issue here is have you experienced His love, and have you become His child? This is our first test question for this chapter.

The absolute highest expression of God's love for us is found at the crucifixion of Jesus. Here at Calvary, God demonstrated pure love by the fact that *"God commendeth his love toward us, in that, while we were yet sinners, Christ died for us* (Rom. 5:8). At the Cross, God's love removed the bondage of yesterday's failures to allow us to transition into today's spiritual provisions and tomorrow's hopes. Freedom happened through Christ's love on the Cross. Enmity with God was eradicated by Jesus' selfless love for everyone at the Cross. The deepest of this love is bestowed upon all true believers. Yes, Calvary should prove even to the most skeptical person that God is not blind to our plight, but that He loves us. The question is, have you experienced it?

What does experiencing the love of the Father look like? In a word, change. The Bible clearly says the truly saved *"should be called the sons of God."* Would there be any greater change available for a person who has transitioned to a son or daughter of God? The Bible goes on with *"therefore the world knoweth us not, because it knew him not."* The truly changed person will be an oddity in this world because he or she will be in the process of conforming more and more into the image of the One the world just doesn't understand (Rom. 8:29).

The person who has truly been saved and has experienced the love of God will be changed. There is no getting around it. Change is the barometer of the influence of God's love upon a person's heart.

Many people who claim to be born again haven't changed though. God's love poured into a heart is not the same as God's love proven to a mind. God's love poured into a heart is a real heart-experience of being loved by God. God's love proven to a mind is the conclusion of an argument, with or without the sweetness of feeling loved by God in the heart. Said another way, in too many people there is information, but there is no transformation. There are many who are informed, yet few who are transformed (Mt. 22:14).

"Beloved, now are we the sons of God, and it doth not yet appear what we shall be: but we know that, when he shall appear, we shall be like him; for we shall see him as he is. And every man that hath this hope in him purifieth himself, even as he is pure" (1 John 3:2–3). Here's the proof of the previous exclamation. Believers are now, unequivocally, a child of God. Not that they shall be; they are at the moment of true conversion. But verse 3 is a key verse. It describes what the change mentioned earlier truly means, which is purity. God wants His children to be like Him. So this is the first step to understanding if you understand the love of God. Are you stirred to live a pure, biblical life because of His love for you?

"Whosoever committeth sin transgresseth also the law: for sin is the transgression of the law" (1 John 3:4). These next four verses are very powerful and not for the faint at heart. They bring us to the second test for this chapter. This test asks the question, "Do you turn away from sin or turn to it?" There has always been, and always will be, a great need for deliverance from the eternal effect of sin on a person's soul. Most people think this refers to the gross sins of society. Because of this, many people think their sins are small and insignificant. But the Bible teaches differently. Everyone will be held accountable and judged based on their sins, large or small. And sin, in a nutshell, is the failure

to keep God's Word. It will be impossible to keep God's Word if one doesn't know God's Word. This is the exact state of affairs for the vast majority of people now. Biblical ignorance is at an all-time high despite the fact we have access to God's Word in ways our parents and grandparents couldn't dream about. The proof is in all of the wrong theology that is propagated in today's world, most of which is terribly wrong and not biblical. Yet people believe it as if it were the gospel.

"And ye know that he was manifested to take away our sins; and in him is no sin" (1 John 3:5). Here is stated the methodology for one's deliverance from sin. When a person truly believes, God counts the sacrifice of Jesus for us personally. Our sins are removed from us and are gone forever. We are now not only free from the penalty of sin, but also from the power of sin too.

Verse 6 is very important as it states: *"Whosoever abideth in him sinneth not: whosoever sinneth hath not seen him, neither know him."* Does this verse really mean what it says? Well, why wouldn't it? Are we to think God would just throw this verse in here to mess with us? No, it is here because it is the truth.

Here is the demonstrable proof of our deliverance. The person who truly abides in Christ turns away from sin, not to it! Their theology is biblically accurate and Christ honoring, not watered down, wrong, and flesh honoring. Can this honestly get any clearer? Biblical theology states here that the person who dwells in Christ will not sin, and the person who does sin has neither seen Jesus nor knows Him. Doesn't that blow the current worldly theological model out of the water? So this particular part of the test is challenging us with truth that, quite frankly, the world chooses to ignore and fluff up. How are you doing on this part of the test?

"Little children, let no man deceive you: he that doeth righteousness is righteous, even as he is righteous" (1 John 3:7). The issue with the modern ideas of biblical theology is that most, if not all, are deceptions. According to the Bible, we can be deceived about the concept of sin and deliverance, too. I submit we have been deceived, and I think our test scores prove it.

What the Bible is actually saying in these four verses is that the one who abides in Christ is one who absolutely does not manifest a lifestyle of continual, habitual, unabated sin. To the contrary, if one continually lives a life of sin, in simple terms, then they don't really know Jesus nor love God. Regardless of what they profess, they, therefore, cannot truly be born again! They may cry *"Lord, Lord"* (Mt 7:22), but they do not continually do the will of the Father in heaven (Mt 7:21).

Reader, do not be deceived! Genuine salvation results in a new creation, a new lifestyle, a new direction. No, it is not *perfection*, but it is a new *direction*! If you are still living in sin after you have made a profession, your profession is useless. The Bible clearly teaches if you are abiding in Jesus you won't be abiding in sin, and if you are abiding in sin, you are not abiding in Jesus. If you are not abiding in Jesus, and He is not abiding in you, you are not saved.

"He that committeth sin is of the devil; for the devil sinneth from the beginning. For this purpose the Son of God was manifested, that he might destroy the works of the devil" (1 John 3:8). Furthermore, the person who is content with sin is said to be of the devil. A person cannot have the Holy Spirit and the spirit of antichrist in them at the same time. Where are you in your faith walk? Would you say you love Jesus and follow Him and His Word continuously? Or are you perhaps content with just getting by and not demonstrating much change in your life. The person who is content with that life is failing the test.

How do I know I really love God? In a nutshell, I will stop loving what He hates.

"Whosoever is born of God doth not commit sin; for his seed remaineth in him: and he cannot sin, because he is born of God" (1 John 3:9). Here is the result of deliverance. The true believer, the one who can truly pass the test, is free from living in and practicing sin. The true believer, according to the true theology of the Bible, cannot and will not continue in sin. According to this verse, the true believer simply doesn't continue to sin because Jesus lives in him, and he is born of God. This is in direct opposition

to what so many in the world currently believe. I ask you now, who are you going to believe and follow? Will you turn from continuous sin, or continue in it? Will you pass or fail?

"In this the children of God are manifest, and the children of the devil: whosoever doeth not righteousness is not of God, neither he that loveth not his brother" (1 John 3:10). Here we are introduced to the third question from the "How Can I Know I Love God" test. Love, or the lack of love, will reveal the true character of a person. In fact, Scripture informs us that based on this characteristic one can determine one's own birthright. Those people who sin continuously and are content to live in a manner that has no concern for other people are children of the devil. This is a very strong statement from God's Word, and I am sure it is quite caustic to those who are challenged by it, but it is right there in black and white. Without the indwelling of God's love via His Spirit, a person cannot love others. If the indwelling of the Holy Spirit is absent from a person, then Jesus has never truly delivered them. If Jesus has never delivered a person, the person is still spiritually dead. If spiritually dead, they are the enemy's children.

"For this is the message that ye heard from the beginning, that we should love one another" (1 John 3:11). This concept of loving others is as old as the Bible itself. There is no new theory here. If a person has trouble seeing the fruit of a loving spirit after an alleged conversion process, the conversion process never happened.

"Not as Cain, who was of that wicked one, and slew his brother. And wherefore slew him? Because his own works were evil, and his brother's righteous" (1 John 3:12). True, biblical love does not persecute the righteous. This verse describes the most severe form of persecution, which is murder. However, if a person has ever wrongfully accused and persecuted another believer, they are just as guilty. I have seen pastors treated like common trash by many so-called born-again people. I have seen others sit by and watch them being treated like that and not come to their defense. I have seen the "blood is thicker than water" mentality as family and friends do the same to innocent church members. If you've ever done anything like this, or supported anyone who has, you have failed this part of the test.

"Marvel not, my brethren, if the world hates you" (1 John 3:13). Here's what the people described above don't realize. The world will hate the person who really loves Christ and people. If you think about it, these people described above are more about the world than they are about the Lord.

"We know that we have passed from death unto life, because we love the brethren. He that loveth not his brother abideth in death" (1 John 3:14). Godly love is the proof that one has passed from spiritual death to spiritual life. It is one of the strongest proofs that one is truly saved. Love is not the cause of us passing from death to life; it is the proof one has. It can't be said any clearer.

"Whosoever hateth his brother is a murderer: and ye know that no murderer hath eternal life abiding in him" (1 John 3:15). Love does not hate. This should be clearly understood, but it is not. Why do so many people feel that they are acceptable to God and that God will never reject them, yet they have all sorts of negative feelings against others? This verse calls them murderers. Jesus took this much further in Mt. 5:21-22. It's not pleasant, but it is important.

Is this teaching new to you? You're reading what the Bible says for yourself, so why should any of this surprise you? If it does, have you been fooled with theology that is not biblical? Think about this: studying the wrong information in order to pass a test won't help you pass it at all.

"Hereby perceive we the love of God, because he laid down his life for us: and we ought to lay down our lives for the brethren" (1 John 3:16). Why did Jesus go to the Cross? Why did Jesus die for sins? Why did Jesus live out His Father's will? Why was Jesus constantly obedient? Because He loved us and He loved His father.

When we are truly saved, that attitude of love will be given to us in the form of the Spirit who lives in us. It should be no surprise that our spiritual personalities would therefore take on the same characteristics Jesus had. We should start noticing a growing and more dynamic love for God and people. If that never has happened, or has died out, we have failed this part of the test.

"But whoso hath this world's good, and seeth his brother have need, and shutteth up his bowels of compassion from him, how dwelleth the love of God in him?" (1 John 3:17). This verse is a practical application of the previous verses. Notice it is a question and not a statement. If a person has the means to help someone, yet does not have the heart to do so, how can that person have the love of God in them? They have failed their test.

"My little children, let us not love in word, neither in tongue; but in deed and in truth" (1 John 3:18). Here, we start the fourth test in this exam. The issue here is do we have a clean heart? Does our talk match our walk? More importantly, does our talk and walk match God's talk? If our hearts are clean, we will be okay; if not, we won't be. A clean heart is made by loving others in deed and not in word only. Unrepentant sin will change a person. They will struggle with compassion and rarely reach out and comfort and help others.

"And hereby we know that we are of the truth, and shall assure our hearts before him" (1 John 3:19). To love only those who love us is to love only in theory and in speech. It is not loving like God loves. When we love others because we love God and His love resides in us, we know we are of the truth or truly saved. If we don't, the strong argument could be made that we are still lost.

How sure are you of your own salvation? Have you passed these tests?

"For if our heart condemn us, God is greater than our heart, and knoweth all things" (1 John 3:20). A clean heart is wrought by God knowing all things. If our hearts condemn us, and they typically do at some point, it's not all bad. In fact, God has made our "new" hearts sensitive so that we will sense wrongdoing. Why? So that we will correct our behavior and not destroy ourselves, that's why.

So, God is greater and knows all things. He knows everything about us, and I do mean everything. He also knows how to assure our hearts and how to give us confidence toward Him. But the pressing issue is the heart *is* deceitful above all *things*, and desperately wicked (Jeremiah 17:9). The human heart a person is issued at conception will always struggle; therefore, God must give us a "new" heart; a spiritual heart. This happens at the moment of conversion inception. Does your "heart" assure you and give you confidence you're in good standing with God? Is that really important? It seems to be to God. Look at our next verse.

"Beloved, if our heart condemn us not, then have we confidence toward God" (1 John 3:21). This verse is self-explanatory and furthers the idea brought up in the previous verse. Through the "heart transplant" we receive from our faith in Jesus, and our desire

to be an above average student who takes His tests seriously and passes them with a high grade, we can be confident that we are in good standing with God. This is the very reason I wrote this book.

"And whatsoever we ask, we receive of him, because we keep his commandments, and do those things that are pleasing in his sight" (1 John 3:22). At first glance, this verse seems to be a continuation of our previous lessons. But it is actually taking the concept of obedience even deeper. A clean heart (also known as a clean conscience) is available only by keeping God's Word and doing the things that please Him. If a child disobeys his or her parent, most parents would be displeased. God, as our heavenly Father, certainly is. The only way a disobedient child pleases his or her father is by obeying him. The same is true with God.

Obedience to God is one of the primary responsibilities of His children. How are you doing on this? Are you obedient rarely? Some of the time? Most of the time? That's failing the test.

"And this is his commandment, That we should believe on the name of his Son Jesus, and love one another, as he gave us commandment" (1 John 3:23). Here is the way to establish a "clean heart." First, our faith and beliefs must become truly biblical, and we must believe in the name of Jesus. Believing in the name of Jesus means believing the totality of Who He is and what He taught.

It is studying His teachings to the point where we know His truths well enough to take and pass our tests.

Next, we must be able to demonstrably prove He is alive in us by the company we keep and the loving care we extend to all people, but especially to other believers.

"And he that keepeth his commandments dwelleth in him, and he in him. And hereby we know that he abideth in us, by the Spirit which he hath given us" (1 John 3:24). A clean conscience is brought forward by the indwelling of God's Holy Spirit. We know we have received a new spiritual heart because the Holy Spirit now operates in the true believer. He guides, nurtures, and encourages us. He disciplines, convicts, and convinces us. He is constant and permanent. He will prompt us to pray, serve, worship, and study. He will always lead us to where Jesus is worshipped corporately and to a closer walk with Jesus. He will help the true believer with growing and maturing spiritually.

Does any of this describe you? If not, why not? Have you failed yet another test? I certainly have in my earlier faith walk. As discouraging as it may be if you have too, there is hope. But we must continue on in God's final exam to uncover our weaknesses if we're ever going to get help.

We continue on with this second test in God's final exam as we go into the fourth chapter of the book of 1 John. This part of the test brings us back to our need for doing something about the nature of false teachers.

"Beloved, believe not every spirit, but try the spirits whether they are of God: because many false prophets are gone out into the world" (1 John 4:1). Once again, the Bible challenges us to be biblically wise and to know God's true theology which is contained in His Word. Notice this verse brings us to the concept that false teachers and their false teachings have a spiritual element to them; a bad spiritual element; an inappropriate spiritual element; a deadly spiritual element.

So, this section helps us to successfully answer the fifth question on how we know that we love God. We know we love God because we are willing to test the spirit of false teachers. John writes to the *"beloved,"* so he is writing to true born-again believers. True believers will always be suspicious of false teachers and should never fall for their false teaching. So, how do we know? The next verse starts us off.

"Hereby know ye the Spirit of God: Every spirit that confesseth that Jesus Christ is come in the flesh is of God:" (1 John 4:2). We are given here the first concept of how we can know if a person is legit or not. The true teacher will confess Jesus Christ openly and unashamedly. He or she will teach true biblical concepts verified by the Word of God. This starts with the incarnation of Jesus– prophesied in the Old Testament and fulfilled in the

New Testament. But that's just the starting point. This must also certainly mean all the facts and truths about Jesus' birth, life, ministry, teachings, death, and resurrection. A true teacher will passionately tell you the truth, the whole truth, and nothing but the truth about the Truth. Why? Because a true teacher is indwelt by the Holy Spirit of God, and they can't help but teach the truth.

A false teacher typically teaches partial truths, or half-truths, and politically correct statements. A false teacher loves to point out alleged errors in the Bible, hard to understand verses, and their own opinions. A false teacher would rather talk about current events, sports, food– anything but Jesus. A false teacher might know all the right words, say all the right things, and sprinkle a little Jesus here or there, but he or she will not be motivated to give Jesus much glory because they typically want the glory all to themselves. Their confessions are self-centered and selfish. Do not be fooled.

"And every spirit that confesseth not that Jesus Christ is come in the flesh is not of God: and this is that spirit of antichrist, whereof ye have heard that it should come; and even now already is it in the world" (1 John 4:3). Ultimately, false teachers are spokespeople for the devil due to their "antichrist" spirit. The Bible teaches the spirit of antichrist has been around for centuries, and, at some point, as it grows in its influence, will usher in the true Antichrist.

"Ye are of God, little children, and have overcome them: because greater is he that is in you, than he that is in the world" (1 John 4:4). Truly born-again Christians have the Holy Spirit in them who will never allow them to fall for false teaching, and because of that, they should overcome it. This is applicable only if they are following the Holy Spirit's leading. If not, they can be easily fooled. If a person is not born-again, he or she can be easily fooled. And that is failing the test.

"They are of the world: therefore speak they of the world, and the world heareth them" (1 John 4:5). Here's the underlying issue: false teachers have worldviews that are not biblical. They sound good. They appear to know what they're talking about. They can be very informative and charismatic, but they are still false teachers. A secular, humanistic, plural, or any other ideological worldview other than a biblical one will absolutely cause a person to become a false biblical teacher.

One of the greatest evils to this is that the world (unregenerate people) loves the worldview of everything and anything as long as it is not biblical. False teachers know this, and they enjoy the notoriety their audience gives them. Christian, do not be fooled, or you will absolutely fail the test.

"We are of God: he that knoweth God heareth us; he that is not of God heareth not us. Hereby know we the spirit of truth, and the spirit of error" (1 John 4:6). The true believer will know a true teacher

just as easily as he or she should spot a false one. One teaches truth; one teaches error. One will prepare their students to successfully pass their tests; one will celebrate when the student fails.

Speaking of tests, how are you doing on this one? Do you follow true teachers or false ones? Do you like those who tell you what you want to hear about yourself or those who tell you the truth? If it's the former, you're setting yourself up for failure. Let me elaborate a bit.

Two thousand years ago, Jesus told other people what they desperately needed to know. It was not very popular, and it ultimately killed Him. Two thousand years later, people are telling other people what they want to hear. This teaching is very popular, but it is actually killing the people.

If you really want to know Jesus and pass your final exam, you must study His teachings for yourself. If you need tutoring, that is okay. Find a true teacher of the Word of God and ask for help. Let us stop getting our theology training from those who have a non-biblical worldview and state things such as, "well, I think …" You want to know what Jesus thinks. You're going to be tested on that.

"Beloved, let us love one another: for love is of God; and every one that loveth is born of God, and knoweth God" (1 John 4:7). These verses

start another test in the bigger exam of how you can know that you really love God, and that is, once again, do you love one another? Love is a predominant theme in the Bible, and I am sure by now you have noticed it. This verse states unequivocally that the person who loves others is born of God (saved) and knows God (passing the test). Since one of God's attributes is His love, and since true believers should start having attributes that reflect God's attribute, the true believer should at some point start reflecting love to others.

"He that loveth not knoweth not God; for God is love" (1 John 4:8). Who is this person who does not know God nor love Him? He or she is the person who lives selfishly, discriminates, steals, neglects others, abuses others and themselves, criticizes, back-bites, gossips, curses, gets angry, hates, murders, character assassinates, sows discord, is divisive, and follows the self-satisfying false teachings of others just like them. This person is not concerned with helping others or showing care for his fellow human. He or she is the person who causes hurt, pain, and suffering. They are failing their tests. Do you know anyone like this?

"In this was manifested the love of God toward us, because that God sent his only begotten Son into the world, that we might live through him" (1 John 4:9). There is a better way to live one's life; a more successful way; a more God honoring way.

God's love has been brought out into the open for over two thousand years. And He clearly states His love offers us new life: a life full of betterment, success, and honor. A spiritual life brought to existence by the death of Jesus' physical life, and the new heart we receive because of His resurrected life. This verse should send shivers down our backs and motivate us to excel at test time.

"Herein is love, not that we loved God, but that he loved us, and sent his Son to be the propitiation for our sins" (1 John 4:10). If the previous verse didn't give you shivers, hopefully this one will. God loved us in spite of the fact that we were not very lovely at all. He loved us long before we loved Him, if we truly do love Him.

The sin nature we all have is the greatest of all false teachers because it will cause us to try to hide from God or run away from Him. But the truth is God loves us in spite of all of that. The proof to that unimaginable love is that His Son Jesus would be His payment for our debt. God paid what we owed because we could not pay it ourselves. We owed a debt. We were imprisoned debtors with no way out. We were to live and die in the dungeon of sin until the arrival of Jesus.

I will study and prepare for any test He requires of me because He is the title holder to my soul. He is the holder of the key to my new heart. He is the faithful and true Jesus. He is the greatest, true teacher in the history of humanity. And His yoke is not burdensome.

"Beloved, if God so loved us, we ought also to love one another" (1 John 4:11). Here is the true believer's last test for this section in a nutshell. Since God loves us sacrificially, and He lives in us, shouldn't we, too, love sacrificially? This is the common sense conclusion to the earlier verses. How are you doing with this?

"No man hath seen God at any time. If we love one another, God dwelleth in us, and his love is perfected in us. Hereby know we that we dwell in him, and he in us, because he hath given us of his Spirit" (1 John 4:12–13). God is not known by sight. He is known by faith and hearing His Word (Rom. 10:17). We can know that we love Him by our faithful hearing of His Word and by the corresponding love we have because of His indwelling Spirit in us.

> *And we have seen and do testify that the Father sent the Son to be the Saviour of the world. Whosoever shall confess that Jesus is the Son of God, God dwelleth in him, and he in God. And we have known and believed the love that God hath to us. God is love; and he that dwelleth in love dwelleth in God, and God in him."* (1 John 4:14–16).

John's own testimony is that the biblical account of Jesus is true, and it should also be every true believer's testimony. This great promise is an offer to the entire human race. In these verses, the Bible records that John knew and believed in God's love. He passed this particular test. Note the three critical things John testified about.

First, God is love, and He sent Jesus to the Cross due to His great love of His creation. Second, true believers must love also because they dwell with Him, and He in them. Third, loving one another is one of the ways we can tell we are saved.

"Herein is our love made perfect, that we may have boldness in the day of judgment: because as he is, so are we in this world" (1 John 4:17). Here, the Bible informs us that our willingness to be used by God to love other people will be made perfect in the sense that we have God's assurance that our love for others will allow us to have security in the day we stand before Him in judgement. At this judgment of Jesus, some will be rejoicing; some will be weeping. It all depends on how we have lived, not what we believed. It depends on what we have done for Him, not what we have said about Him.

So, how do you think you will fare in this particular exam setting?

"There is no fear in love; but perfect love casteth out fear: because fear hath torment. He that feareth is not made perfect in love" (1 John 4:18). If a person truly loves someone, he or she will not be afraid of

them. Godly love casts out all fear. There is no such thing as a heart full of love and hate. It is impossible. So, anyone who says they love God would never run and hide from Him out of fear. They will seek Him. They will study about Him. They will deal with their sins through Him. God's love, living in the new heart of regenerate people, will be attracted to God in ways that would keep them from doing anything short of passing His tests with flying colors. Is that you?

"We love him, because he first loved us" (1 John 4:19). As we begin to understand God's true love for us, we fall deeper in love with Him. It's only natural for us to love someone who loves us the way God does.

"If a man says, I love God, and hateth his brother, he is a liar: for he that loveth not his brother whom he hath seen, how can he love God whom he hath not seen?" (1 John 4:20). This is another powerful verse that grades our performance. Once again, the person who talks but doesn't do is called a liar. I wonder how many so-called Christians have failed this part of the exam. I wonder how long they're going to be content in doing so as they call out how Jesus loves them.

"And this commandment have we from him, That he who loveth God loves his brother also" (1 John 4:21). Here, we are informed that loving others is a commandment. It is because when we don't, we should be convicted of our lack of spiritual vitality. The

person who claims to love God (they claim to be saved) should have a supernatural love for all people– at least to the point where they do not want to see anyone die and go to hell.

So the truly saved person will evangelize, or at the very minimum, provide support to those who do. He or she will support their local church in its efforts to spread the gospel. He or she will help the true teachers as they teach the truth to those in darkness. He or she will make every effort to advance the cause of Christ to the uninformed. He or she will lead others away from false teachers and will recognize them when they see them. He or she will have and maintain a worldview that is honoring to the Lord. Is that you?

How Can I Really Know I Really Love God?

Test Two of God's Final Exam
1 John 3:1–4:21

Be very honest with your answers. A help would be to answer them the way you think Jesus would answer them about you!

YES NO

1. Have I really experienced God's love for me?

2. Do I consistently turn from sin or to it?

3. Am I marked by God's love?

4. Do I really have a clean heart?

5. Do I really turn from antichristian teachings?

6. Do I really love others?

Divide your yes responses by 6. This will give you your numeric grade for this test.

91–100% = A Great Job!
81–90% = B Not Bad!
71–80% = C Needs Improvement
61–70% = D Remedial Classes
0–60% = F Not good at all

4

TEST 3 - DO I REALLY BELIEVE IN GOD?

Almost everyone I have ever met claims they believe in God. I have met very few atheists (there is no God) or agnostic (there is a God, but you can't know him) people. No, just about everyone I have ever met has claimed to believe in God. But the vast majority of these people don't really believe in the God of the Bible, or at least not His true attributes. Many believe He's kind of a Santa Claus type of person— full of love and joy and presents. Others believe He is a mean tempered hothead just waiting to get His hands on poor little us. Still, others believe He's a bumbling old busybody who serves no real purpose here in this world.

There are many religions in this world, and they all claim their God is the true God. Who is right? Whose belief and ideas about God are correct? If there is a God, can He be all the various gods of man's multitudes of religions? If these gods were similar to each other, maybe the world religions could pull this off. But these gods are so incredibly different that they can't possibly be the same entity. Humanity's gods range from the benevolent, push-over Santa Claus type to the mean and hateful "I'm gonna get you if you mess up" type. Can these be one and the same? I would think not.

One thing is for sure: if God really exists, then it is of the utmost importance that we are correct in what we believe and think about Him. We must not fall for false teachings; we must stand firm in our search for truth, and we must search diligently.

So how can we tell if we believe in God? How do we know our beliefs and concepts of God are accurate? This is the subject matter of our last test in God's final exam: do I really believe in God? So let us begin in our study preparations.

"Whosoever believeth that Jesus is the Christ is born of God: and every one that loveth him that begat loveth him also that is begotten of him" (1 John 5:1). Being "born of God" means to be spiritually alive. It is a spiritual birth, a rebirth of one's spirit. It is a new heart and life, but just as important, a new behavior and attitude. It is often described as being born-again. It is very familiar to most people as describing one being saved. It is conditional on the person's belief that Jesus truly is our salvation. Therefore, a person must

truly know all he or she can about the life, ministry, teachings, death, and resurrection of Jesus Christ.

God's Word is so deep and powerful concerning the theology of the new birth, or salvation. Because it is so important, let's now look at what the Bible says about this most incredible doctrine.

First, the new birth is a necessity. A person will never see nor enter heaven nor live forever with God unless he or she is born again (John 3:7). No matter what a person feels like or thinks the Bible is crystal clear on this.

Second, once a person is truly saved, there is a new power and spirit in his or her life. It is not the reformation of the person's old nature, it is the actual creation of a totally new person spiritually (Jn. 3:5-6; 2 Cor. 5:17; Eph. 2:10).

Third, salvation is a definite and real experience. Jesus was and is very real. His death, burial, and resurrection were very real. His activity within a truly born-again person is very real. To say one is saved yet there is no real activity of God in their lives is a dead giveaway they are not really saved. Without an intimate influence of the Holy Spirit in the life of a person, that person is still lost, no matter what creed they recited or what ordinance they keep. Without the successful implementation of the next verse in the life of a person, all the professions one makes are just idle babbling.

Fourth, the new birth is a totally changed life. A totally changed life is the proof one is truly saved. Make excuses all you want. Say you're just a sinner saved by grace as your method of not being held accountable for your lack of knowledge and obedience. None of the excuses we all like to use will hold up to the most basic scrutiny of Scripture and God's judgment.

According to God's Word, a truly born-again believer, one who is truly saved from an eternity separated from God, will exhibit the following characteristics daily:

First, he or she will be concerned with living righteously, daily (Eph.2:10). Second, he or she will not practice sinning, daily (1 John 3:9; 5:18).

Third, he or she will love others, daily (1 John 4:7).

Fourth, he or she will not be worldly, daily (1 John 5:4).

Fifth, he or she will keep the faith, daily (1 John 5:18).

Sixth, he or she will possess the Holy Spirit, daily (1 John 3:9; 1 Peter 1:13; Col. 1:27).

"By this we know that we love the children of God, when we love God, and keep his commandments.\" (1 John 5:2). The Bible teaches us repeatedly what the world wants us to deny and forget which

is biblical knowledge and obedience. For a person to say they are saved, but not know and live obediently to all of God's teachings, is the height of hypocrisy.

"For this is the love of God, that we keep his commandments: and his commandments are not grievous" (1 John 5:3). Here again is that repetitive teaching found throughout the Bible. A truly saved person will always be obedient to God's Word. Now, the devil certainly understands this, so he tries to adulterate and dilute the Word using various methods, all of which fall under the heading of false teaching. If he can get you to stumble here, he knows you won't experience the true power of God nor be in a daily relationship with Him. If that happens, he can easily fool you into believing God is not real, or He doesn't care about you. As we're having our pity party, he is leading you further and further away from your true source of help.

The enemy and the world want you to believe God's Word is outdated and antiquated. They want you to believe we are too smart now to need His Word. They want to fool you into believing their way is the best way. So, how do you suppose that is working out?

"For whatsoever is born of God overcometh the world: and this is the victory that overcometh the world, even our faith" (1 John 5:4). If you are truly born again, you have and will overcome the enemy's and the world's lies. God's Word is more important today than

ever. In it, we learn what we need to know about God, His Son, our situation, and the cure. Its pages contain thoughts from the very mind of God. Why wouldn't we want to know what the Bible says? Why wouldn't we want to be obedient to God's Word? Why would we ever listen to and fall for anti-biblical rhetoric? We wouldn't, if we were truly saved. So why are so many Christians falling for the rhetoric? Well, there can only be one answer. They are failing the test too.

"Who is he that overcometh the world, but he that believeth that Jesus is the Son of God?" (1 John 5:5). Overcoming is intrinsically tied to belief. Belief is intrinsically tied to faith. Faith is intrinsically tied to "hearing the word of God" (Rom. 10:17). The person who is lost will never overcome the world. The person who is carnal and disobedient will never overcome either. The person who truly believes in Jesus will demonstrate the changed life mentioned earlier. This is the only life that God empowers to overcome the world and its challenges and influences.

You say you're definitely not overcoming? Then it boils down to a faith issue. Truly saved people will always be people of great faith, and they will always be overcomers. The way may not be easy or pleasant, but they will always overcome it. And the greatest overcoming is passing from death to life, from the temporal to the eternal. God's people are guaranteed this. Why? It's because this verse says so.

Truly saved people have saving faith in Jesus Christ. They know His Word and Him well enough to overcome the false doctrines this world teaches about Him. Truly saved people will always live obedient lives to Him according to His Word. They will also overcome the temptations of this world and their own propensity to sin because of it.

How have you done on this test?

"This is he that came by water and blood, even Jesus Christ; not by water only, but by water and blood. And it is the Spirit that beareth witness, because the Spirit is truth" (1 John 5:6). Here, we begin the second part of the testing procedure for the exam titled "How Can I Know I Truly Believe in God?" The question here is do we truly believe in the biblical witness about Jesus Christ? This is so important that the Bible separates this into two sections. This is part one of those two sections. We will learn about part two when we get to verses 9-15.

Is Jesus the true Christ? The Bible declares beyond a shadow of a doubt that Jesus truly is God's chosen Messiah. The water described here refers to Jesus' public baptism at the start of His earthly ministry. At His baptism, the Spirit of God came upon Jesus in the form of a dove to signify God's approval (John 1:32-34). God then vocally proclaimed Jesus to be His Son (and therefore the Messiah in Mt. 3:17).

The mention of blood refers to His death. It is by His death our sins are forgiven. It is by His shedding of His blood that our judgment and punishment are taken from us by His sacrifice. Because of His death, we are free *from* sin, not free *to* sin. The truly saved get this; the unsaved get it backwards. The truly saved understand the Spirit's witness to them concerning these truths. The unsaved cannot fathom the depth of this truth.

"For there are three that bear record in heaven, the Father, the Word, and the Holy Ghost: and these three are one" (1 John 5:7). Here we are confronted with the concept of the Trinity. The Father, Son, and Holy Spirit are all witnesses to the truth, and they have shared it with humanity. The Father proclaimed Jesus as His Son. Jesus proclaims He is the Son. The Holy Spirit proclaims Jesus is the Son. All three are in total agreement with one another. And if Jesus is the Son of God, that makes Him the only sacrifice sufficient enough to satisfy God's holy demand for righteousness from people.

"And there are three that bear witness in earth, the Spirit, and the water, and the blood: and these three agree in one" (1 John 5:8). The Bible testifies that the supernatural world agrees that Jesus is the Son of God and therefore the Messiah (verse 8). Now the Bible testifies the natural world agrees with that too. Both worlds agree and have only one common message to share: Jesus is the Messiah of both worlds. Since this is true, what more proof do

we need? How much more testimony can one receive beyond that of both the spiritual and physical worlds?

Do you believe in the total deity of Jesus Christ and His finished work on the Cross? Has it changed you, or are you still the same? If you're still the same, how can you truly be saved?

"If we receive the witness of men, the witness of God is greater: for this is the witness of God which he hath testified of his Son" (1 John 5:9). Here we begin part two of believing the witness of Christ. Do we really believe in God? We can test ourselves by studying Scripture.

It stands to reason that God's witness would far outweigh man's witness on anything. Whatever God says must be true, otherwise He's not God, or at least not much of a god. But God's testimony of His Son is accurate and true if for no other reason than God said it.

Humanity has been trying to discredit God's Word since before the ink dried on its pages. Why? It's because if the Bible is true, then we are in serious trouble. Our pride and arrogance want to deny this. Humanity wants to be in control. People want to have the final say so. This is why secularists believe religion hinders people. It is why humanists believe people can fix their own problems. It's why pluralists believe the answers are found in the largest groups. And the list goes on. But the underlying issue with all worldly focused ideologies is the attempt to discredit or totally do away with God. So, we must ask ourselves, which ideology do we really believe?

"He that believeth on the Son of God hath the witness in himself: he that believeth not God hath made him a liar; because he believeth not the record that God gave of his Son" (1 John 5:10). The true believer will make the decision to believe the Bible and follow God as He has described because it is an easy decision to make. When a person has been truly saved, he or she will have the witness of the Holy Spirit within them. Since the Holy Spirit's witness is Jesus is the Son of God and the Messiah, it stands to reason the person full of the Holy Spirit will feel likewise. There shouldn't be any confusion in the mind of the truly born-again person. There should not be any worldly ideological influences in the way a saved person lives and conducts his or her life in this world. If one truly believes, they should have this witness and a life that proves it. Is this you?

"And this is the record, God hath given to us eternal life, and this life is in his Son" (1 John 5:11). Life is another great doctrinal theme in the Bible, specifically eternal life. Eternal life is the opposite of perishing. I see many people who believe they have eternal life, yet they are perishing in this life. You see, eternal life is the cessation of spiritual decay and corruption. It is the stopping of spiritual deterioration. How is it possible to see so many people, who genuinely believe they have new spiritual life, decay and

weaken spiritually? They live, act, think, and respond in ways that are not biblical. If the Holy Spirit truly lived in this person, would He not try to correct him or her? Wouldn't there be some sort of push towards obedient change? Would the Holy Spirit just allow them to continue on in this inglorious lifestyle? The answer to these questions is found in our next verse.

"He that hath the Son hath life; and he that hath not the Son of God hath not life" (1 John 5:12). No. The answer is unequivocally, no. The truly saved person must, by definition, have received Jesus and His life as exchanged for their deadness. When people are unchanged, uncaring, insensitive, rebellious, and disobedient, they are probably unregenerate too.

"These things have I written unto you that believe on the name of the Son of God; that ye may know that ye have eternal life, and that ye may believe on the name of the Son of God" (1 John 5:13). John did not write our final exam to anger or aggravate us; he wrote it to help us see where we truly are in our own self-assessment of our salvation. He wrote it so we may know what God says about us and our walk with Him, not what we think or what the world wants to lead us astray in.

"And this is the confidence that we have in him, that, if we ask anything according to his will, he heareth us:" (1 John 5:14). Our confidence in anything is found only in Him, as this verse teaches. When we are truly saved, our prayer life will be more concerned

with praying God's will than it will be for praying for more materialistic stuff. When you pray, do you pray for the lost, or for more of something you want?

"And if we know that he hears us, whatsoever we ask, we know that we have the petitions that we desired of him" (1 John 5:15). But only if it is asked according to His will. What really is God's true will? Well, for this test, it's that no man should perish (live eternally in hell). That's it. And it begins our next test in determining if we really believe in God. Look at verse 16.

"If any man sees his brother sin a sin which is not unto death, he shall ask, and he shall give him life for them that sin not unto death. There is a sin unto death: I do not say that he shall pray for it" (1 John 5:16). How can I know I truly believe in God? Well, are we living free from sin? Yes or no? That is one of the surest ways. But God goes even deeper here. Do we pray for other believers as they live in sin? Do we engage with them and lovingly confront them about their sins? Do we bring it to their attention? Do we lovingly let them know? Or do we, by our silence, teach them we're fine with it?

Here is the connection: if a person is praying for another person who is living in sin, it is proof he or she is concerned about sin, and, therefore, living righteous lives is important to them. Have you prayed for those you know who are living in sin? Are you regular in doing so? No? You are once again struggling with this test.

"All unrighteousness is sin: and there is a sin not unto death" (1 John 5:17). So, how do we live free from sin? The short answer is by keeping ourselves from it. How do we do that? We do it by understanding two very important concepts.

First, we must be truly born of God. A person, who thinks he or she is saved but really is not, will never be able to accomplish this. Why? Well, because a person must keep themselves under the illumination of Jesus and the light of His Word. Both of these cannot happen if salvation is just an idea and not a reality for a person. This book has been written, in part, to help a person determine if he or she is really saved. By now we should be able to understand why this is important.

Second, we must know that *all* unrighteousness is sin. *All* of it. There is not a single act of unrighteousness that is not sin. Unfortunately, so many people think too lightly of sin. They rationalize that their sins are just not that bad. But the Bible teaches all sin is bad and will cause a person great issues with God. Here, the Bible alludes to sinning unto death. The only sin unto death is to deny Jesus as Savior, of which millions of people are guilty. A person who does that has no recourse for any sin. But there is also the concept of sinning to the point where a person becomes so hardened to God and His conviction of sin, that they no longer even feel conviction anymore. They have persisted in sin and are now too engulfed in sin that it borders on sin unto death.

The point to all of this is that the way we live free of sin is to know what sin is according to God's Word and to stay away from all of it. Does this describe you? If not, why not? It can't be done, you say? Then why does the Bible teach that it can? There must be something deeper involved here.

"We know that whosoever is born of God sinneth not; but he that is begotten of God keepeth himself, and that wicked one toucheth him not" (1 John 5:18). And here it is. The Bible, once again, teaches that a truly saved person will not sin. Now, either the Bible is correct and accurate, or it is not. What do you think?

When we look at the Bible in its entirety, we see the concept that those people who are truly born again will not make it a practice of sinning. It also teaches that Jesus will keep them from the advances of the devil. I've heard many people say, "the devil made me do it," as if that was all the excuse they needed for their friends to look the other way. Here, the Bible proclaims if a person is truly born of God, he or she will not sin, and the devil cannot have any sway over him or her. So, how are we doing on this part of the test?

"And we know that we are of God, and the whole world lieth in wickedness" (1 John 5:19). So now we are confronted with another great theological conundrum: a person is either of God or of the world. A person is either of righteousness or evilness. A person is either of the Kingdom of God or the kingdom of Satan. What this ultimately means is that the world is in opposition to God. Since the fall of humanity, the world has been opposed to God and His plans. It always will be until God takes the world back. And He is going to return to do that in one fell swoop soon, but for now He's doing it one person at a time.

So, how does the true believer live free of sin? By knowing the opposition that lays in front of him or her and by not being fooled by the wickedness of the devil and his dominion. Is that you?

"And we know that the Son of God is come, and hath given us an understanding, that we may know him that is true, and we are in him that is true, even in his Son Jesus Christ. This is the true God, and eternal life" (1 John 5:20). How does a true believer live free of sin and thereby know that they believe God? He or she does so by receiving spiritual understanding given to them by Jesus. I hope He uses this book to assist you.

To truly know that you believe in God is to truly understand the spiritual element of life. This is the only information you must master in order to be truly delivered from sin. Understanding other areas of life just won't get the job done. Deliverance is not found in knowing and understanding emotions, psychology, sociology, philosophy, medicine, technology, or any other human-centered subject, as great as these subjects may be. Deliverance is only found in God's Word and God's plan, and a person must absolutely understand both in their entirety in order to fully understand salvation in any mature form. Is that you? If it is not you, why isn't it?

"Little children, keep yourselves from idols. Amen" (1 John 5:21). How do we keep ourselves free from sin, and thereby know that we believe God? By keeping ourselves free from idols. Interestingly, this closes the book of First John. If we are ever going to know that we believe in God, we must eliminate and eradicate all idols in our lives. Why? The Bible teaches God will not tolerate competing against them for your loyalty and attention.

But what is an idol? An idol is whatever we treasure more than God; whatever drives our thoughts and actions becomes an idol, and these idols dull our spiritual hearing and harden our hearts to things of God. Essentially, an idol can be anything that takes the place of God as the most important focus and priority in our life.

Some modern day examples of idols are self, security, approval, relationships, success, wealth, health, food, intellect, comfort, rest, recreation, peace, joy, happiness, and aloneness. To be sure, these issues are the idols to millions of people, but the greatest idol for many people today is the false Jesus.

What is the false Jesus? He is the idol millions want to believe in. He is all love and no wrath. He is all forgiveness and will never hold a person accountable. He is the god of looking the other way and no discipline. He is the god people flock to because he allows them to sin with no repercussions. He is the laid back and easy going god of people's imagination, not the God described in the Bible. He is the favorite version of Jesus taught by the world, but he is an idol from the mind of the truly misinformed and unregenerate.

In 2 Corinthians 11:3, Paul warns his reader with the following: *"But I fear, lest by any means, as the serpent beguiled Eve through his subtlety, so your minds should be corrupted from the simplicity that is in Christ."* This is exactly what has happened today as the enemy has concocted a false Jesus that millions idolize because the false Jesus is what they want.

How about you? Does the world's rendition of Jesus sound attractive to you? Do you like being told what you're doing right instead of what you're doing wrong? Are you pleased that Jesus has forgiven all your sins, so you're not disturbed when you do sin? Are you content with just being a sinner saved by grace? Are you appalled at the prospect that Jesus' Word might actually say what it says? Has the study of Scripture in this book got you angry or upset? Are you fighting with the biblical Jesus compared to the false Jesus?

You may have an idol in your life. And if so, it is additional proof you are failing the test.

How Can I Really Know I Believe in God?

Test Three of God's Final Exam
1 John 5:1-21

Be very honest with your answers. A help would be to answer them the way you think Jesus would answer them about you!

                                                    YES NO

1. Am I truly born again?

2. Do I truly believe the witness about Jesus?

3. Does my life prove I live free of sin?

Divide your yes responses by 3. This will give you your numeric grade for this test.

100% = A Jesus will be proud!
66% = F Failure
33% = F Serious remedial work is needed
0% = F Talk to your pastor

FINAL EXAM SCORE: Take the cumulative grade of your three separate tests by adding your three test scores together, then divide by three. Your grading scale is below:

91-100% = A Great Job!

81-90% = B Not Bad!

71-80% = C Needs Improvement

61-70% = D Remedial Classes

0-60% = F Not good at all

EPILOGUE

So how did you do on your test? Are you content with your results? Would the Teacher Jesus be content? No? Well, let me assure you, there's hope. To be honest, this book is not designed to bring about shame or ridicule; rather it is a tool to help us understand better where we truly stand with Jesus and if there are weaknesses in our walk with Him, and if so, to determine what those weaknesses are and address them biblically. I have endeavored to do that, and I pray I have accomplished my goals.

As we have learned, John stated with clarity the purpose of his first letter. He proclaimed the good news about Jesus to the recipients of this letter, saying *"so that you too may have fellowship with us; and indeed our fellowship is with the Father, and with His Son Jesus Christ"* (1 John 1:3). Later, John added *"so that you may not sin"* (2:1) and *"so that you may know that you have eternal life"* (5:13). John wanted his readers to experience true fellowship with God and with God's people. But he knew that would not happen until the Christians set aside their own selfish desires in favor of the pursuits God had for them.

To help them attain that goal, John focused on three issues: the passionate zeal of the believers, believers standing firm against false teachers, and reassuring the Christians that they have eternal life. John wrote to churches full of people who had struggled with discouragement, whether due to their own sinful failures or the presence of false teachers in their midst. John hoped to ignite the zeal of these believers so that they might follow the Lord more closely and stand firm against those who meant to sow discord among the churches. In doing so, they would solidify their relationship with God and gain confidence in His work in their lives.

We all go through ups and downs in our Christian faith. Whatever the struggle we face, whether outside of us or inside of us, we often feel ourselves blown about by the winds of emotion or circumstances. Yet God calls us to lives of increasing consistency, with the evidence of our inner transformation becoming more and more apparent as the months and years pass by. How would you characterize your relationship with God? Would you describe it as consistent and fruitful or sporadic and parched? At times, all of this is common. But our relationship with God should be growing towards full maturity and experience in spite of the set-backs. It takes knowledge of God's Word to accomplish this, which leads to action, perseverance and victory.

John knew that we would never find in ourselves the faithfulness God requires. Instead, we have to place complete trust in the work and grace of God, believing that He will certainly conform us to the image of His Son, Jesus. That sense of being grounded in God only comes when we set aside our sin in the pursuit of the one true God. Or, in the words of John, *"if we love one another, God abides in us, and His love is perfected in us"* (1 John 4:12).

May your love for and fellowship with God increase exponentially as you understand your spiritual weaknesses and allow God to direct you to greater fulfillment of your life with Him. May you understand how sin ruins everything, and how Jesus has come to give us a way back in spite of sin. May your love for others demonstrate the changes God has and will accomplish in your life on your journey. May you be ready for Him as your final exam day is approaching.

Lastly, may our King be glorified in our change. Amen.